WALK AROUND

A-6 Intruder

By Lou Drendel

Walk Around Number 2
squadron/signal publications

Introduction

During my research for this book, I was hanging around the VA-65 maintenance spaces at NAS Oceana when one of the Senior Chiefs came up with a quote, which says more about (a) the remarkable A-6 Intruder and (b) the current state of the U.S. military, than the thousands of words which have been written about both subjects. He stated, "I have been working on this airplane half my life, and now we are getting rid of it, just when it is better than it has ever been!" The Chief was about thirty-five years old, so it is doubly ironic to consider that the A-6 Intruder was born about the same time as he was!

The extraordinary career of the A-6 has spanned years which saw an explosion of technology, from vacuum tubes to solid state integrated circuits, from low frequency radio ranges to satellite global positioning systems, from dumb bombs to smart bombs, and finally, to plastic wings! As awkward and ungainly as it looks, the airframe of the Intruder has accommodated all of these changes with equal aplomb, proving conclusively that "Pretty is as Pretty does". The fact is that the Intruder is more mission-capable today than it has ever been, which is testament to the genius of it's designers. The Intruder is also a member of another very exclusive club. It is one of a very few U.S. military aircraft which have never been exported or sold to a foreign power. It has only been flown operationally by the U.S. Navy and U.S. Marine Corps. It has distinguished itself in combat in Vietnam, the Gulf of Sidra and the Persian Gulf. It stood the cold war watches which ultimately led to victory in that long and costly conflict.

Sadly, by the time you read this the A-6 Intruder will be gone. The cost-cutters have come to Washington, and the military is suffering at the hands of those who do not subscribe to the doctrine that preparedness is the ultimate deterrent. There is no dedicated replacement for the

ISBN 0-89747-327-2

If you have any photographs of aircraft, armor, soldiers or ships of any nation, particularly wartime snapshots, why not share them with us and help make Squadron/Signal's books all the more interesting and complete in the future. Any photograph sent to us will be copied and the original returned. The donor will be fully credited for any photos used. Please send them to:

Squadron/Signal Publications, Inc.
1115 Crowley Drive.
Carrollton, TX 75011-5010

Acknowledgments:

U.S. Navy	U.S. Marine Corps
Ted Carlson/Fotodynamics	Dave Mason
Jim Sullivan	Dr. J.G. Handelman

Intruder. It's mission will be assumed by a combination of F/A-18s and F-14 "Bombcats". As sleek and supersonic as they are, they will not match the load-carrying capability and deadly precision of Grumman's premier attacker.

A pair of new production A-6A Intruders of VA-42, the East Coast replacement aircrew training squadron. Both aircraft carry external fuel tanks on the outboard wing pylon.

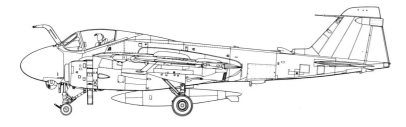

Grumman A-6E (TRAM) Intruder

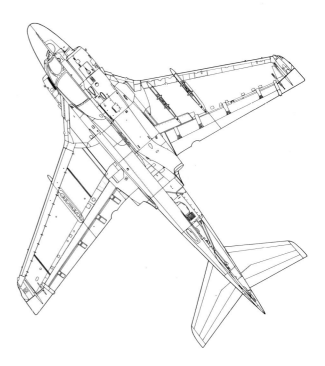

The final attack variant of the Intruder was the A-6E TRAM. This A-6E of VA-42 was on final approach to NAS El Centro, California on 15 January 1994. VA-42 remained the East Coast crew training squadron throughout the operational life of the A-6.

The nose gear door has the landing light mounted in the center of the door, along side this light are the three carrier landing signal lights.

The nose landing gear strut has the catapult tow bar attached to the front. The large circular object attached to the right side of the strut is the hydraulic nose wheel steering mechanism.

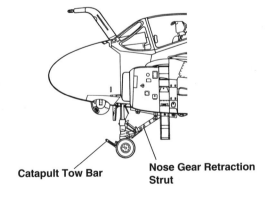

Catapult Tow Bar

Nose Gear Retraction Strut

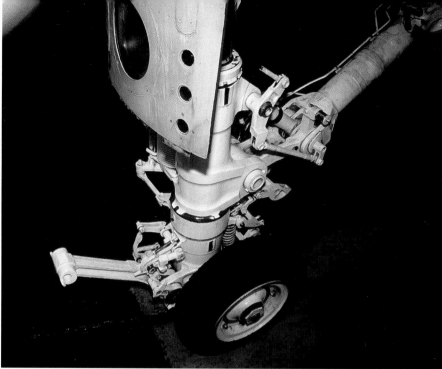

The port side of the nose wheel door has the carrier landing system lights. The LSO is able to tell if the aircraft is fast (Green, top light) on speed (amber, middle light) or slow (red, bottom, light) as it approaches the carrier deck for an arrested landing.

This A-6E is hoisted on jacks for landing gear maintenance. The stabilizing oleo scissors link is fully extended. The Black lines running down the retraction strut are nose wheel steering hydraulic lines.

The catapult tow bar is in the raised position. When the aircraft is positioned on the catapult the bar drops down and engages the catapult shuttle. Once the aircraft is released from the catapult, the bar returns to the raised position.

The nose gear doors fit snugly against the bottom of the air intakes on the A-6E. The large light in the center of the small nose gear door is the landing light.

The nose landing gear well of an A-6E. The interior color is Gloss White, which is used as a maintenance tool, because things like hydraulic fluid leaks will be very visible against it. The edges of the gear doors are Red.

There are only very slight differences between the nose landing gear of the A-6A through A-6E variants and the nose landing gear of this EA-6B Prowler.

An A-6A of the Weapons System Test Division, Naval Air Test Center, NAS Patuxent River, at NAS Glenview, IL during May of 1969. There are few external differences between models of the A-6. This aircraft has an AN/ALQ-100 ECM antenna on the leading edge of each outboard pylon.

The built-in crew boarding ladders on either side of the aircraft are Red, as are the intake splitter plate and edges of the landing gear doors.

The TRAM turret sensor windows are, left to right; laser designator, Forward Looking Infrared (FLIR), and laser receiver.

This is the stowed position of the A-6E TRAM turret. When in the stowed position the turret is rotated 180 degrees so that the sensor windows are protected from damage while the aircraft is parked.

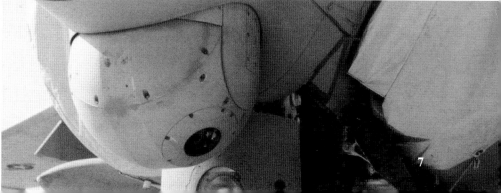

The laser receiver lens (right) is more visible in this view of the TRAM turret. The large lens is the Forward Looking Infrared (FLIR) camera system. The turret can rotate 360 degrees, and can also pivot downward to track targets as they get closer to the aircraft.

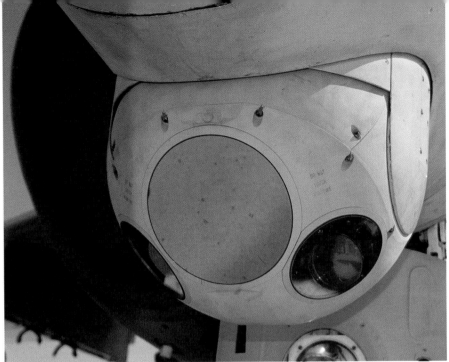

The turret system allows the sensors to remain locked onto a target as the A-6 maneuvers to drop bombs. The TRAM turret can be slaved to the radar crosshairs on the BN's multi-mode radar set.

TRAM is an acronym representing Target Recognition and Attack Multi-sensor. The turret itself is twenty inches in diameter. TRAM was introduced to the A-6 fleet during 1979.

The radome has been swung open on this A-6E TRAM for servicing of the AN/APQ-156 multi-mode radar. The interior of the radar bay is White, while most of the "black boxes" are in fact, Gray.

The avionics equipment trays swing out to allow easy access to black boxes on both sides of the radome.

This is the same avionics equipment tray as above, but viewed from the rear.

With the radome raised, the avionics tray can be folded out for easy access. There is another fold out avionics tray on the other side of the radar bay. The interior of the radar bay is in Gloss White, while most of the avionics boxes are Gray.

At least four wiring bundles are visible when viewing the avionics tray from the side. The rack holding the Gray avionics boxes is Natural Metal.

An A-6A Intruder of the Marine Intruder training squadron, VMAT(AW)-202, being prepared for a mission from MCAS Cherry Point, North Carolina on 20 July 1972. The aircraft has Red Foreign Object Damage (FOD) screens over the intakes and starter carts hooked up.

A-6As and A-6Es were painted with Gloss Gull Gray uppersurfaces over Gloss White undersurfaces during the 1960s and 1970s. VMAT(AW)-202 was disestablished on 30 September 1986.

A KA-6D tanker at the moment of launch from the bow catapult aboard USS AMERICA during November of 1985. The nose gear catapult tow bar has dropped down and engaged the catapult shuttle.

Port engine air intake on an A-6E. The rectangular plate in front of the intake is the boundary layer splitter plate.

The open radome reveals the large multi-mode radar scanner and smaller intermediate frequency receiver (long "egg crate") under the scanner.

The external power receptacle is on the starboard side of the A-6, just behind the crew boarding ladder.

The canopy actuating mechanism is located behind the open access panel to the right of the crew boarding ladder compartment .

The external refueling panel is located in the same compartment as the external electrical power receptacle. The refueling of all A-6 tanks, including external tanks, is controlled from this panel.

13

Part of the pre-fight check is the cycling of all control surfaces and nose gear extension/depression. Signals for all movements are given to the pilot by the Plane Captain, who monitors all movements and indicates with a "thumbs up" signal when all are operating properly.

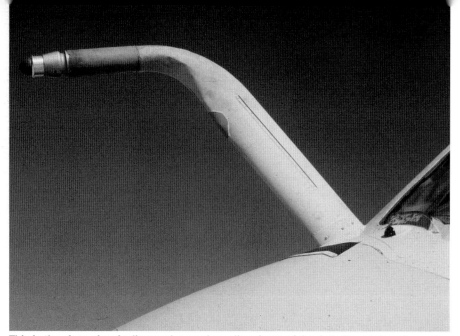

This is the air-to-air refueling probe used on all variants of the A-6. Naval aircraft use the probe and drogue method of aerial refueling, in contrast to the Air Force which uses the boom method of refueling.

The A-6 has no internal APU or method of self-starting the engines. External air is necessary and it is the responsibility of the Plane Captain to connect the starter cart hose to the engine receptacle.

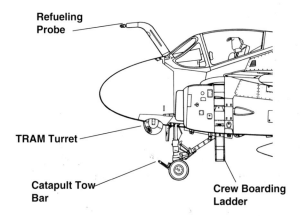

Refueling Probe

TRAM Turret

Catapult Tow Bar

Crew Boarding Ladder

The engines can not be started simultaneously, but either engine can started first. Once the engines are running, one of several ground crewmen who assist in the pre-flight will disconnect the external air hose and secure the access panels on both sides of the fuselage.

The pilot and/or the Bomb/Navigator (BN) will check the status of the refueling panel switches during their pre-flight walk around.

Small hydraulic jacks are used to support the nose of the A-6 when undergoing maintenance to the nose gear and related systems.

The starboard boarding ladder is used by the Bombadier/Navigator (BN). The underwing panel has been removed to service the aircraft's air conditioning unit. The large air intake at the wing root supplies ambient air for the environmental control unit.

A KA-6D Intruder tanker is directed to the bow catapults aboard USS AMERICA (CV-66). Once in place, the catapult tow bar will drop down and engage the catapult shuttle, which will propel the aicraft down the catapult track once the signal has been given to launch. The aircraft is carrying four external fuel tanks. The tanker can transfer the fuel from these tanks as well as the internal fuel tanks.

The engine air intake on this EA-6 is covered with a Gray fabric protective cover that also covers the intake splitter plate. The Red crew boarding ladder is in the lowered position, although both cockpit canopies are closed. The engine cover has the squadron identification, VAQ-129, on it in Black against a White background.

The canopy on this A-6E (BuNo 152895, NH 510 of VA-95) is securely buttoned-up while the aircraft was on the ramp at NAS Miramar on 24 April 1993. The canopy on the A-6 series went unchanged until the advent of the four place EA-6B. The A-6 canopy provides excellent visibility for both crewmen.

This A-6E of VA-145 has a Green air intake cover with the squadron identification in Yellow. The aircraft carries twenty-three fuel pump markings (indicating buddy refuelings) on the engine bay in Black. The square at the bottom of the Rescue arrow is White with a Yellow border. On it are printed instructions on how to release the canopy.

A-6E (BuNo 162211) side number AD-555 (side number displayed as three [triple] nickels on nose) of VA-42, on approach to NAF El Centro, California on 13 March 1992. The canopy provides the pilot with excellent visibility to the side, but this wide area of glass makes him somewhat vulnerable. Flak curtains were installed on some A-6s to provide a measure of side protection for the pilot and BN.

The post antenna for the Automatic Carrier Landing System (ACLS) is located under the nose, just to the rear of the TRAM turret and offset slightly to starboard on the A-6E .

The metal bar running across the inside of the canopy of this A-6E (BuNo 161662) of VA-85 is the brace for the flak curtain. This aircraft was one of the A-6s that took part in the Libyan raids and may have had the flak curtains installed at that time.

Engine bleed air is used to blast rain and/or ice from the windscreen. It is directed upward from this row of vents mounted at the base of the windscreen. The small fairing just forward of these vents is the refueling light which shines on the refueling probe during night refueling operations.

This small triangular window divides the left and right portions of the main windscreen. This window was common to all A-6 variants.

The object in the center of the danger markings on the port side air intake is the Angle of Attack (AOA) sensor.

The temperature probe is located on the starboard engine air intake, immediately above the push-in hand grip.

The canopy on the A-6A through A-6E slides to the rear controlled by the hydraulic piston visible at the rear of the open canopy.

All KA-6s have been retired. Those not in storage at Davis Monthan AFB are used as maintenance trainers, such as this example at NAS Fallon, BuNo 151819, formerly of VA-165. A number of interesting items are visible, including detail of the wing fold area, lowered refueling hose housing, boarding ladder and fuselage speed brake. The open panels on the fuselage are part of the engine access area.

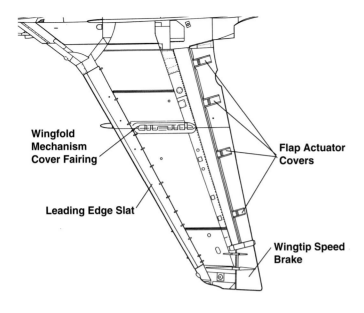

Wingfold
Mechanism
Cover Fairing

Flap Actuator
Covers

Leading Edge Slat

Wingtip Speed
Brake

The bulge in the center of the wing is the wingfold mechanism cover fairing. This is one of the composite-winged A-6Es.

Also visible on the wing uppersurface, besides the wingfold mechanism fairing, are the flap actuator covers and ECM fairing just behind the outboard wing fence and the fuel dump outlet, which is below the ECM fairing.

An A-6E (BuNo 161671, WK 510) of VMA(AW)-224 in the landing pattern at MCAS El Toro, California on 26 April 1991. The aircraft has the wing leading edge slats and trailing edge full span flaps fully extended. The wingtip speed brakes are in the closed position, however, when the aircraft turns onto final approach, they will be deployed.

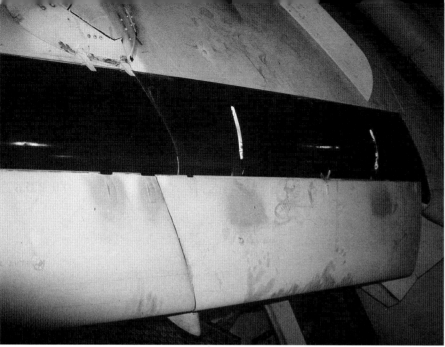

The leading edge slat in the fully open position. The interior of the slat and the wing area under it are in Red. There are NO STEP legends on the slat in Medium Gray. The bulge at the top left is the wing fold mechanism cover fairing. The darker spots on the slat are areas of fresh paint. The Gray camouflage paints used on the A-6s did not weather well and fresh paint often stood out.

The wing fold mechanism cover fairing on the older metal winged A-6s is much smaller and is not as smooth and drag free as the new cover on the composite wing. Additionally, this wing has no fuel dump at the wingtip.

In the closed position, the leading edge slat fits snug with the top of the wing. The boundary layer wing airflow fence helps direct the airflow over the control surfaces at the trailing edge of the wing.

The new composite wing has two boundary layer air flow fences used to direct airflow over the trailing edge control surfaces. Speed brake actuator fairings are outboard of the small fence at the right.

23

There is a speed brake mounted on each wingtip. The actuators are covered with aerodynamic fairings on both the top and bottom of the speed brake. These are very effective in slowing the aircraft and are used routinely during landing approaches. Outboard of the speed brake is a low intensity strip formation light.

The wing leading edge slat in the fully entended postion. The slat is controlled by two actuators visible in the White areas. Also above each actuator are White "Caution" warning legends.

This A-6E has the upper wing spoilers and trailing edge flaps fully extended. The spoilers are immediately forward of the full span trailing edge flaps on the uppersurface of the wing. The spoilers are used to dump lift and enhance braking effectiveness on landing rollout. The aircraft is also carrying Multiple Ejector Racks (MERs) on the inboard underwing pylons. The MERs are configured with Blue twenty-five pound practice bombs.

The interior of the wingtip speed brake is Red with a White warning legend. Immediately to the right of the speed brake is a low intensity formation light. On the left side is the fairing for an Electronic Countermeasures (ECM) antenna. Directly under the ECM fairing is the fuel dump vent.

This A-6E of VA-42 was opened up for routine maintemance at NAS Oceana, Virginia. The interior of the flap track is in Red.

Environmental control system ram air intake is the larger of the two air scoops visible on the upper rear fuselage. The smaller scoop at the left is a cooling air intake for the avionics bay.

The emergency Ram Air Turbine (RAT) is extended from the rear of the port wing root to provide emergency electrical power in case of an engine failure.

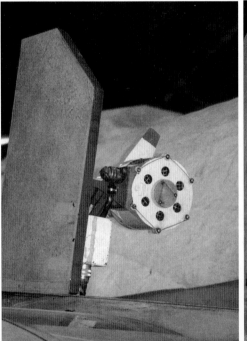

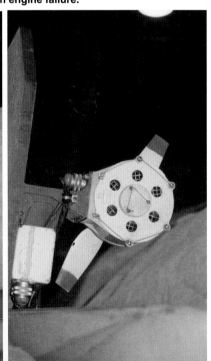

An A-6E (BuNo 155637, NJ 811) of VA-128 on final approach for landing at MCAS El Toro, California on 22 April 1988. The wingtip speed brakes are fully delpoyed to allow the pilot to keep the engines spooled up at higher power settings in case he needs to make a missed approach and go around. The interiors of the leading edge slat, speed brakes and flaps are in Red. The landing gear legs are fully extended with their oleo pistons at the full travel position.

An A-6A aboard USS KITTY HAWK (CV-63) during December of 1968. The aircraft is taxiing with the wings folded, a normal practice aboard ship where space is always tight. The aircraft also has ECM antennas on the leading edge of the outboard underwing pylons. The White external fuel tanks both carry the squadron number on the nose in Black.

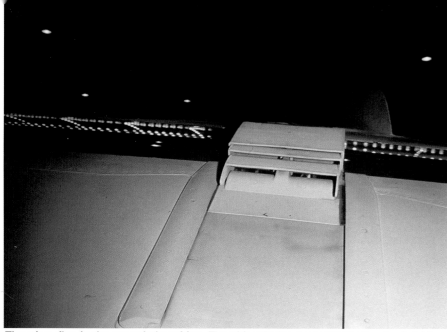

The wing flap in the extended position. The object in the center is the flap track fairing. Full span flaps are extended to 20 degrees for both takeoff and landing.

The upper fuselage of the A-6 has several air scoops. The large scoop is for the environmental system ram air intake, while the smaller scoop forward on the fuselage is a cooling air intake for one of the avionics bays.

The wing flap in the retracted position. Visible are the flap track fairing (center) and boundary layer wing airflow fence.

The cooling air spill vent is located under the canopy rail on the port side of the aircarft.

The underside of the wing showing the leading edge slat and slat control access panel.

The large bulge under the wing tip leading edge is the antenna for the ALR-45 radar warning receiver. The fairings on the wing trailing edge are the acuators for the wing tip speed brake. Immediately next to the ALR-45 fairing is the Red port position light. There is also a small White light positioned on the wing leading edge, above and to the left of the position light.

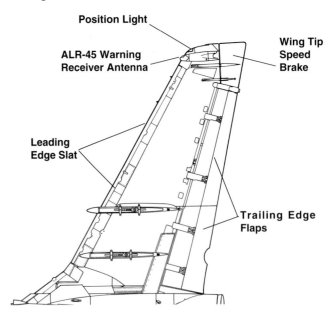

Position Light

ALR-45 Warning
Receiver Antenna

Wing Tip
Speed
Brake

Leading
Edge Slat

Trailing Edge
Flaps

The wing leading edge slat is fully extended. The inside of the slat is painted Red. The slats are extended and retracted by the hydraulically operated screw in the center.

The outboard main landing gear door actuator mechanism. The hydraulic piston on the actuator is extended. All gear door operating parts and the interior of the doors themselves are painted Gloss White to show fluid leaks. The door edges are in Red.

Visible at the forward edge of the landing gear well is the air conditioning system exhaust fairing, which is stainless steel. The fairing is made of steel because it can get extremely hot.

The outboard main landing gear door (port side) viewed from above. One of the required items to check on a preflight check is the condition of the hydraulic lines running to the door actuators.

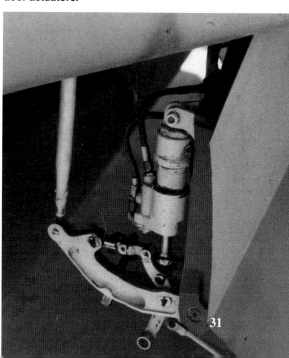

The fairing over the wing leading edge above the main landing gear well contains a communications antenna.

The interior of the main landing gear wheel well is a mass of hydraulic, electrical, pneumatic and other lines. The interior of the wheel well is Gloss White.

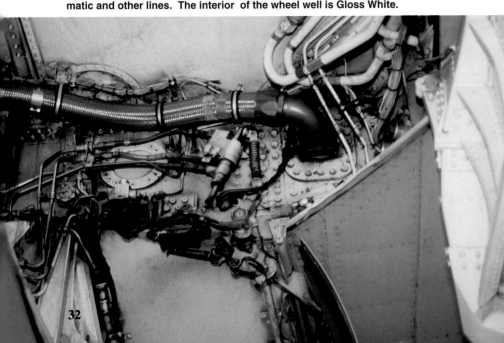

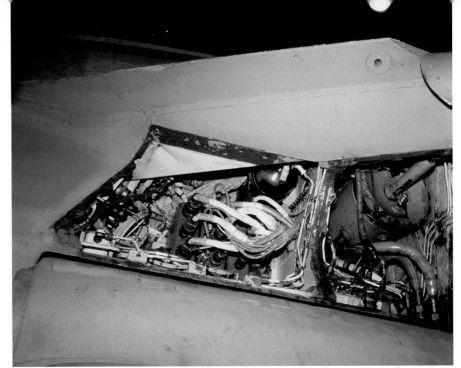

The knife edge fairing on the wing leading edge next to the fuselage is a stall warning buffet strip. The open access panel is for the navigation computer.

When the flaps are deployed, the flap acutator on the underside of the wing slides out of the actuator fairing.

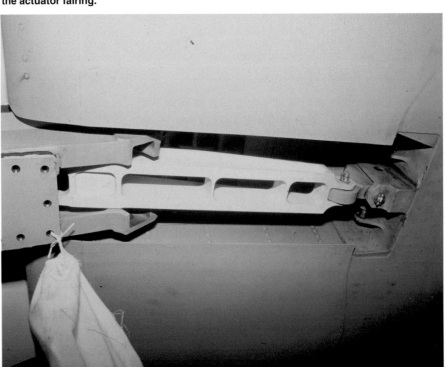

Main landing gear wheel well (inboard is at top, forward is at the left). The landing gear retracts forward and the wheel rotates to lay flat within the wheel well.

The large intake on the starboard wing root is for the aircraft's air conditioning system. Next to it is the starboard wing stall warning buffet strip. The bright fairing at the bottom is the air conditioning air exhaust port.

The trailing edge flaps can be extended some twenty degrees for landings and takeoffs. The object in the foreground is the flap actuator/guide. Also visible is the trailing edge of one of the underwing ordnance pylons.

A Marine A-6E (ED 403, BuNo 161689) of VMA (AW)-533 on approach to Nellis AFB, after returning from a Red Flag mission on 23 August 1989. The aircraft is carrying Multiple Ejector Racks (MERs) on the outboard pylons and a range instrumentation pod on the starboard inboard pylon. The port MER has a Blue twenty-five pound practice bomb in place on the forward outboard rack. The landing gear on the A-6 retracts forward, with the wheel rotating to fit flat in the wheel well. The fuel tank under the fuselage is a 300 gallon tank. This same tank can be carried on the wing pylons as well.

Late production A-6E TRAMs were fitted with a rearward facing Electronic Countermeasures (ECM) antenna and fairing on each wing. The antenna was mounted at the juncture of the full span flaps and wingtip speed brakes. The fuel dump vent is located under the ECM fairing on each wing. These ECM fairings were originally developed for the A-6F program and later retrofitted to the A-6E under the Stand Off Weapons program.

The large underwing leading edge fairing is the antenna for the Radar Homing And Warning (RHAW) receiver. The fairings in the foreground are the wingtip speed brake actuator fairings.

Inboard fuselage area near the main landing gear well. The large White object is the main landing gear sidestay and breaker strut.

Late production A-6E TRAMs were fitted with a rearward facing Electronic Countermeasures (ECM) antenna and fairing on each wing above the fuel dump vent. These ECM fairings were originally developed for the A-6F program.

The main landing gear well door (inboard is at the top). The door retraction mechanism is at the right. The interior of the door is in Gloss White.

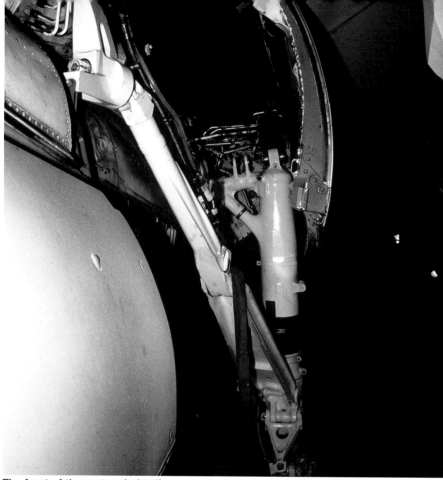

The front of the port main landing gear strut, strut attachment point and retraction arm. All landing gear parts are painted Gloss White.

The main landing gear attachment point is at the left and the landing gear retraction strut is at the top.

The starboard main landing gear wheel well door, looking forward. The door retraction arm is in the center, along with the retraction system hydraulic actuator.

Main landing gear strut with the aircraft tie-down chains attached to the tie down attachment points. Each wheel strut, mains and nose, have these tie down points.

This is the port main landing gear leg of an EA-6B. It is identical to the landing gear used on other variants of the A-6 series. The data plate on the main strut provides maintenance personnel the information such as the part serial number, when the strut was made, oleo pressures, and other valuable information.

This A-6 is suspended on jacks for landing gear drop checks. The Natural Metal main landing gear oleo strut is fully extended.

The wing flap cut out is to accommodate the underwing tank. It was discovered that when the flaps were lowered they struck the wing tank. The cut out prevents this from happening.

There are two main landing gear attachment points. The pivot point on the left is much larger than the one in the center. The landing gear must be made this strong since it must withstand landings at very high sink rates, as must all naval aircraft.

Looking back along the fuselage underside from the nose wheel well, there are a number of vents, engine compartment cooling air scoops, and a Red anti-collision light. The centerline pylon is configured with a 300 gallon external fuel tank.

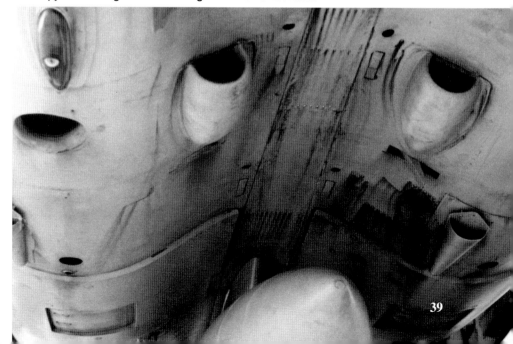

The inboard weapons pylon has the lower covers removed revealing the interior of the pylon. The wing pylons on the A-6 are stressed to carry up to 3,600 pounds. The two inverted V shaped objects are bomb/fuel tank sway braces, which help to hold the bomb/fuel tank steady on the rack. The plugs hanging down are electrical connectors that connect the pylon with whatever type of rack is suspended from it. The pylons are also plumbed to receive 300 gallon external fuel tanks. The Red flag on the main landing gear strut is a Remove Before Flight marker for the landing gear locking pins.

This is the original wing fold mechanism used on all metal winged A-6 aircraft, including EA-6s. The wing fold joint is even with the outboard underwing weapons pylon. The wings fold hydraulically and can be folded or spread from the cockpit without outside assistance. With the wings folded, the wing span is reduced by more than half, making storage on the carrier far easier. There are four locking lugs visible on the upper portion of the fold. The wing fold mechanism actuator is the V shaped object in the center .

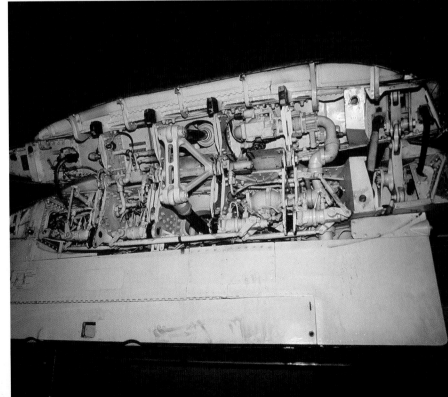

An A-6E TRAM (NK 500, BuNo 157000) of VA-196 at NAS Miramar, California on 5 December 1992. This aircraft was retrofitted with the new composite materials wing configuration. This retrofit was easily identified by the White cylinder in the wing fold mechanism.

The composite wingfold on an A-6E. In an attempt to prolong the service life of the A-6, a new composite material wing made of graphite, epoxy, titanium and aluminum was manufactured by the Boeing Defense and Space Group in Wichita. The original plan was for all Intruders to be rewinged, but the decision to retire the A-6 from active service cut the plan just short of getting the entire fleet rewinged.

The wing fold is even with the outboard weapons pylon. This A-6E has a Penguin Mk 3 anti-ship missile hung from the pylon. The Penguin missile was developed by Norway and is used on their F-16s. It was selected by the U.S. Navy for use on the SH-60B Seahawk helicopter and is built for the Navy by Grumman. It has a range of 25 miles and can be used by fixed-wing aircraft, such as the A-6.

An A-6A (BuNo 152587) of VMA(AW)- 221 chocked and tied down on the ramp at MCAS Cherry Point, NC on 13 April 1971. The aircraft has tie down chains running from just the main landing gear struts, the nose wheel does not have tie downs attached.

The wing fold mechanism has four locking lugs at the top of the fold. The hydraulic V shaped actuator is visible in the center of the fold.

42

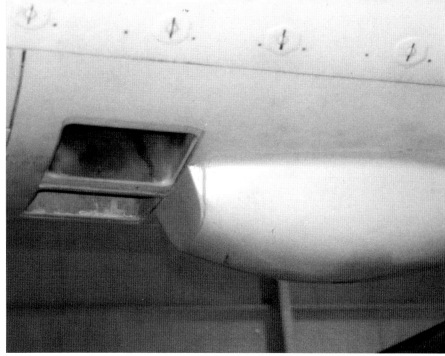

The Doppler radar radome (starboard side) and MX-7721/ALE-29A Chaff/Flare dispenser ports are located under the mid-fuselage, just ahead of the tail hook.

The small under-fuselage radome houses an APN-153 Doppler navigation radar antenna. This radar is used to provide navigational update information for the inertial navigation system.

The underside of the rear fuselage with the tail hook in the stowed position. The two square ports are the MX-7721/ALE-29A Chaff /flare dispenser ports and the five points protruding downward from the fuselage are the radar beacon antenna system.

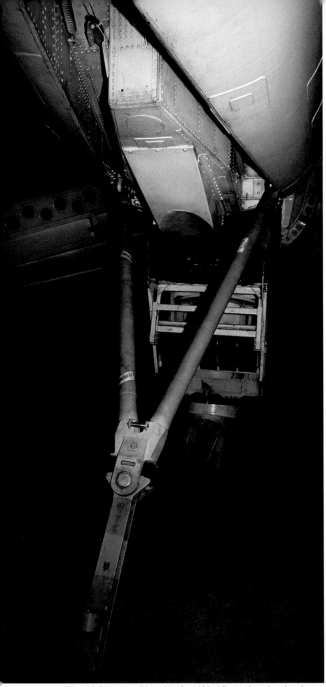

The Y frame tailhook of a KA-6D tanker in the lowered position. The curved fairing in front of the tail hook is the hose guide for the Hose/Drum refueling unit.

The tail hook of an A-6E in the stowed (left) and lower (right) positions. The fairing in front of the A-6Es tail hook is the Doppler radar housing, which was deleted in favor of the Hose/Drum unit on the KA-6D at left. The hook is painted in Black and White stripes to make it more visible to the carrier's Landing Signal Officer.

The open access panel above the lowered tail hook of this KA-6D houses Electronic Countermeasures (ECM) transmitters.

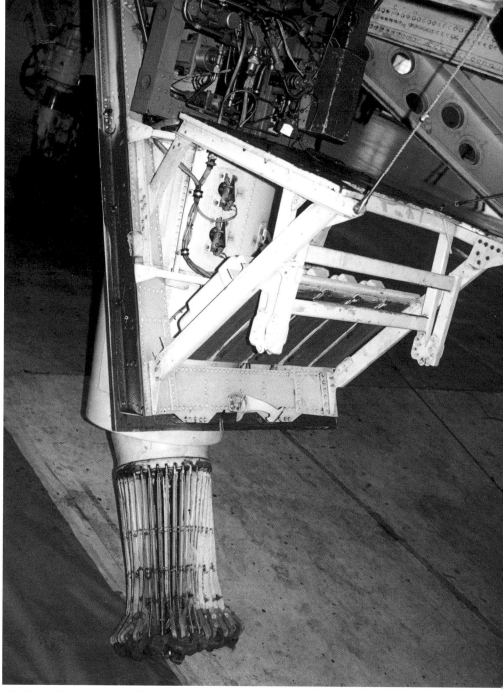

The Extensible Equipment Platform on the KA-6D is hinged at the forward end. This platform contains the refueling Hose/Drum unit. The object at the bottom is the refueling basket that trails below and behind the KA-6 during refueling operations.

The Extensible Equipment Platform of the A-6E is hinged at the rear. It holds avionics equipment, a video recorder, Chaff/Flare Dispenser controls and a maintenance ladder for servicing the Intruder's Liquid Oxygen System, which is in the fuselage just forward of the avionics bay. The mechanic holds the Green LOX bottle which will be installed before the aircraft is released for flight.

The A-6E does not have fuselage-mounted speed brakes. An equipment bay takes the place of the speed brakes mounted on early A-6As. Normally it is covered by a solid access panel.

This large ram air scoop on the A-6E is for avionics cooling in the rear equipment bays. The circle at the bottom of the "Y" is the arresting gear hydraulics reservoir sight gauge and the hole under the insignia is a cooling air exhaust vent.

The Extensible Equipment Platform of an A-6E Intruder with the LOX bottle installed.

The leading edge of the A-6E fin contains the Remote Compass Transmitter as well as communications antennas and the pitot tube. The anti-collision light just under the pitot tube is Red on standard aircraft and Green on aircraft equipped with night vision goggles.

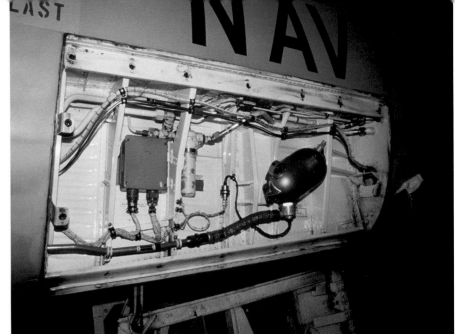

The port side fuselage equipment bay on an A-6E Intruder. The interior of the bay is Gloss White. This bay occupied the area that was taken up by the fuselage mounted speed brakes on the A-6A. When the speed brakes were relocated to the wingtips on the A-6E, the area was then given over for equipment storage, including the fire extinguishing system supply bottle.

The starboard equipment bay has a foil covered pipe running through it along with various hydraulic and electrical lines and control valves. The Extensible Equipment Platform is visible just below the open bay.

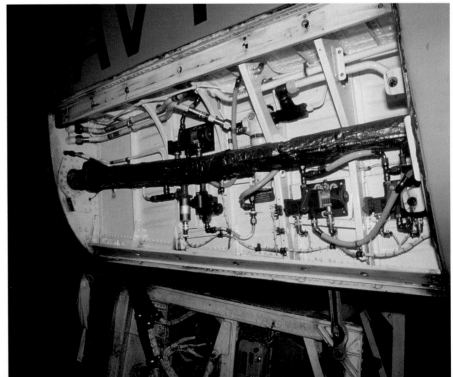

The port side fuselage equipment bay and lowered Extensible Equipment Platform on an A-6E. The legend below the fire extinguisher system bottle reads, " Service If Presure Is Below 100 PSI." The Danger warning cautions against connecting electrical lines until the bottle is secure and the discharge lines are connected.

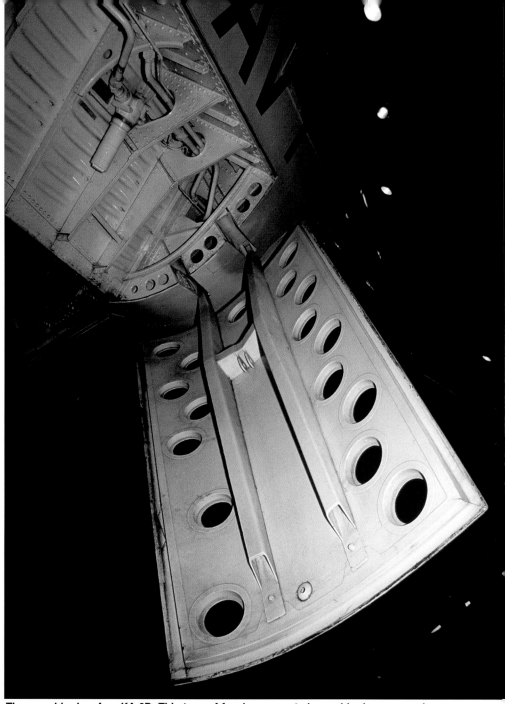

The speed brake of an KA-6D. This type of fuselage mounted speed brake was used on early A-6s, although problems with the speed brake often led to them being wired shut.

The fin of the A-6E contains a rearward facing Electronic Countermeasures (ECM) antenna in the streamlined fairing just above the rudder. The fin cap itself contains a UHF Identification Friend Foe (IFF) antenna.

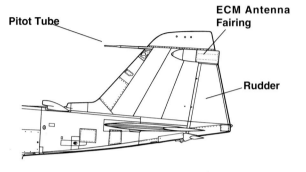

Pitot Tube

ECM Antenna Fairing

Rudder

The lower portion of the extreme rear fuselage contains the rear White tail navigation light at the base of the rudder. The vent at the left is the fuselage fuel tank jettison pipe.

The EA-6B vertical fin is topped by a large radome containing self protection and communications jamming equipment receivers and transmitters. The protrusion at the rear of the radome is the radar warning antenna. There is a strake at the bottom of the rudder to smooth the airflow and eliminate flutter.

The rear fuselage, fin and tail planes of an A-6E. The fin tip houses a rearward facing Electronic Countermeasures (ECM) antenna in the streamlined fairing just above the rudder, while the fin cap itself contains a UHF Identification Friend Foe (IFF) antenna. Just below the rudder is a White position light. On the fin leading edge is a anti-collision light mounted just below the pitot tube boom. The leading edge of the fin cap has a communications antenna built into it. Just below the horizontal stabilizers is the fuselage fuel dump pipe. This is used to jettision fuel prior to landing if the aircraft is too heavy to come aboard the carrier. At the forward base of the fin is the rear fuselage venting air intake.

The tin tip of the EA-6A housed the AN/ALQ-86 receiver/surveillance system, AN/ALQ-41 I and J band track breaker and AL/ALQ-100 self-protection system. Additionally, the EA-6A retained the fuselage mounted speed brakes used on early A-6As. Most EA-6As were used by the Marines, like this aircraft of VMCJ-2 at MCAS Cherry Point, North Carolina. On the EA-6A the pitot tube was relocated from the fin to the port wing.

The rear fuselage fuel dump vent on the A-6E is located at the base of the fin. It allows the quick dumping of fuel so the aircraft can get down to landing weight if it returns to the carrier with excess fuel. Landing weight is critical on aircraft carriers and dumping fuel is the method used to control the aircraft's weight.

This open access panel on the starboard rear fuselage reveals the stabilator control linkage on an A-6E.

These open access panels on the port rear fuselage are for (front) ECM transmitter/receivers and (rear) control linkages.

The centerline pylon on the A-6 can be used to carry ordnance or fuel tanks. Most commonly, it is configured with a 300 gallon fuel tank.

The refueling basket used on the KA-6D. The lights above the basket are the fuel flow status lights that tell the receiving pilot that fuel is flowing through the hose.

The Hose/Drum unit is mounted on the Extensible Equipment Platform and the basket is housed in a streamlined fairing when not extended. The KA-6D also retains the fuselage speed brakes.

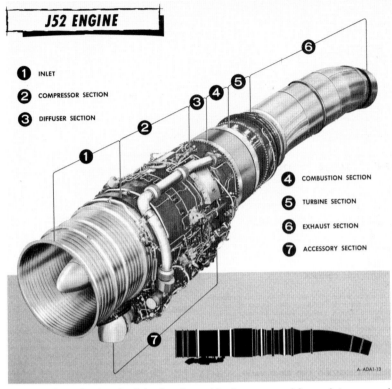

J52 ENGINE

1. INLET
2. COMPRESSOR SECTION
3. DIFFUSER SECTION
4. COMBUSTION SECTION
5. TURBINE SECTION
6. EXHAUST SECTION
7. ACCESSORY SECTION

A-ADA1-13

This A-6E engine has had the fuselage skinning removed for maintenance of the engine exhaust.

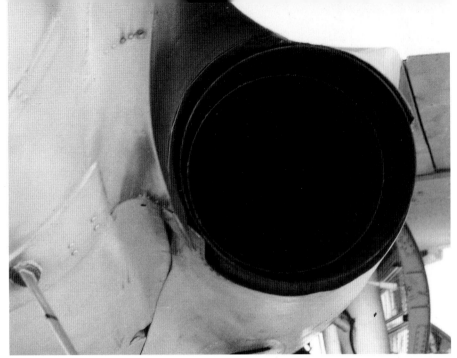

A-6E engine exhaust area. The blade antenna at the left is for the UHF communications system.

The engine compartment of an A-6E with the access panels fully open and strut locks in place.

A J-52 engine rests on an engine maintenance stand under an A-6A, in position to be installed in the engine compartment . The J-52 was used throughout the career of the A-6 with little change or modification to the engine.

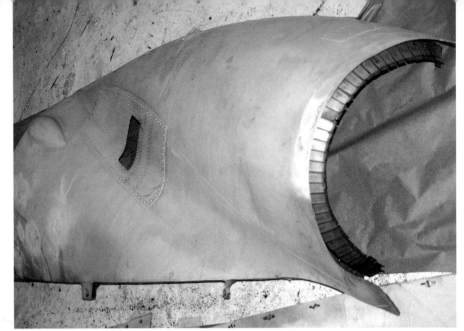

The rear fuselage (exhaust) fairing removed during maintenance. When in place, this fairing covers the engine exhaust section except for the extreme end of the exhaust pipe.

Engine intake of the J-52 engine. The compressor section turbine blades are visible behind the bullet fairing.

The starboard side of the J-52 engine compartment, with a J-52 installed, (looking rearward). The external power (air) receptacle is at the right.

The port side of the J-52 engine compartment (looking rearward). The engine compartment access doors are hinged at the top.

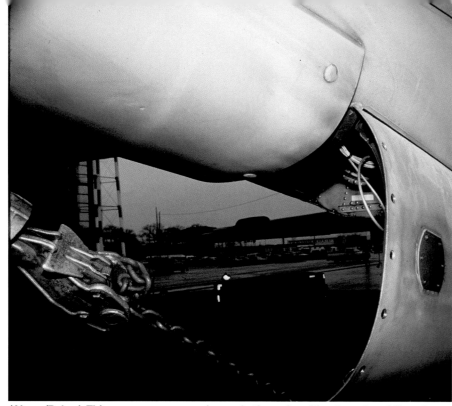

(Above/Below) This open access panel reveals the radar altimeter set and its antenna (the thin wafer on the access panel exterior). The unit itself and various electrical connections are on the interior of the hinged panel.

When performing maintenance on the landing gear, the weight of the aircraft is supported by these maintenance jack stands.

The EA-6B is a four place aircraft with side-by-side seating for its crew. The separate cockpits each have their own canopy. The crew boarding ladder remains the same as on earlier A-6s, with a platform to assist the front cockpit crewmen in boarding the aircraft.

A pair of EA-6B Prowlers of VAQ-131 aboard USS CONSTELLATION on 7 March 1994. The EA-6B is primarily a jammer platform, although it can carry and fire the HARM anti-radiation missile.

The fairings on either side of the EA-6B fin are for Band 1 and Band 2 transmitter antennas. The fin cap contains self protection and communications jamming equipment.

The refueling probe of the EA-6B differs from the standard A-6 series in that it is offset to starboard. The crewmen are seated in Martin-Baker GRUEA-7 ejection seats.

This EA-6A of VMCJ-2 at MCAS Cherry Point has the engine compartment open, the Extensible Equipment Platform lowered and the speed brakes deployed.

An EA-6A undergoing carrier qualifications. The first flight of the EA-6A was on 26 April 1963. The aircraft is configured with underwing jammer pods and three 300 gallon fuel tanks.

A-6E cockpit, the pilot is on the left side and the bombadier/navigator is on the right, slightly lower and further back than the pilot. The BN's cockpit is dominated by the large radar scope and tactical displays. The control stick on the BN's console is for rapid control of the weapons system. Using this stick, the BN can boresight the radar on a particular target, then slave the TRAM turret's sensors to this same traget.

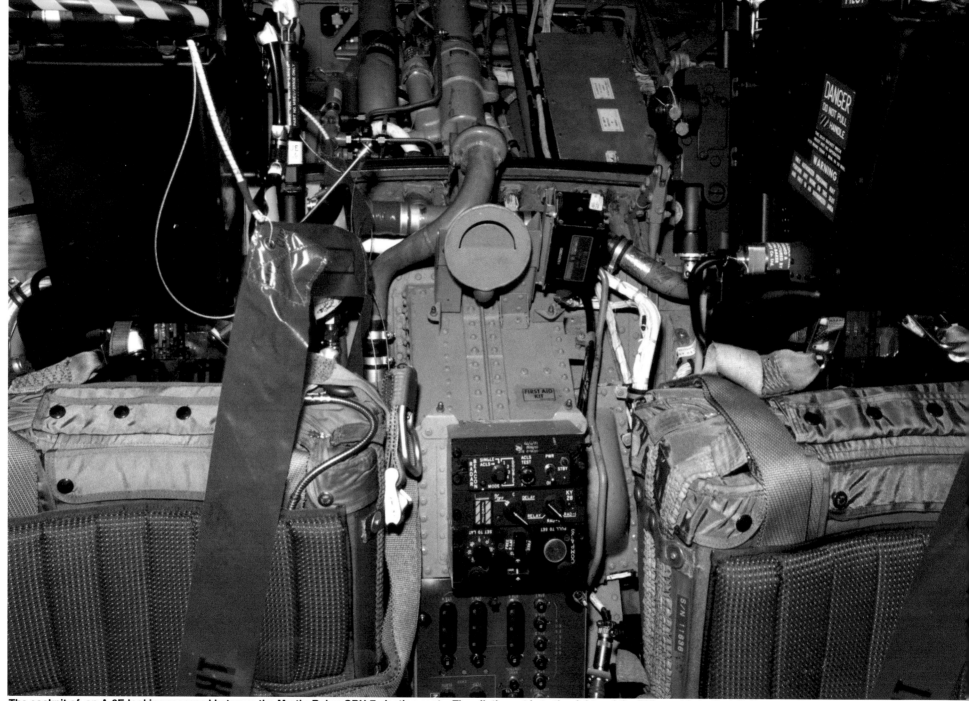

The cockpit of an A-6E looking rearward between the Martin-Baker GRU-7 ejection seats. The pilot's seat is to the right and tbe BN's seat is to the left. Between the seats are the controls for the radar beacon, radios, and radio compass. Both seats have "Red Remove Before Flight" banners attached to the seat safety pins.

The instrument panels of an A-6B Intruder. The A-6B was used for the Iron Hand (anti-SAM missile) mission and had enhanced threat identification electronics and the capability to fire the Standard and HARM anti-radiation missiles. The pilot had a radar repeater scope in front of him, as well as an optical sight mounted above the instrument panel.

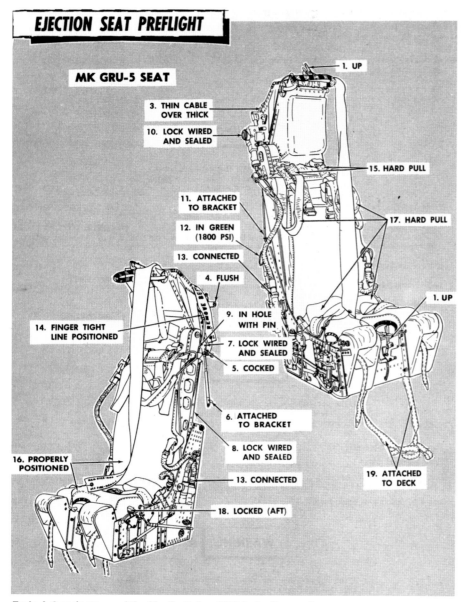

MK GRU-5 SEAT

1. UP
3. THIN CABLE OVER THICK
10. LOCK WIRED AND SEALED
15. HARD PULL
11. ATTACHED TO BRACKET
12. IN GREEN (1800 PSI)
13. CONNECTED
17. HARD PULL
4. FLUSH
1. UP
14. FINGER TIGHT LINE POSITIONED
9. IN HOLE WITH PIN
7. LOCK WIRED AND SEALED
5. COCKED
6. ATTACHED TO BRACKET
8. LOCK WIRED AND SEALED
16. PROPERLY POSITIONED
13. CONNECTED
19. ATTACHED TO DECK
18. LOCKED (AFT)

Early A-6 variants used the Martin-Baker GRU-5 ejection seat.

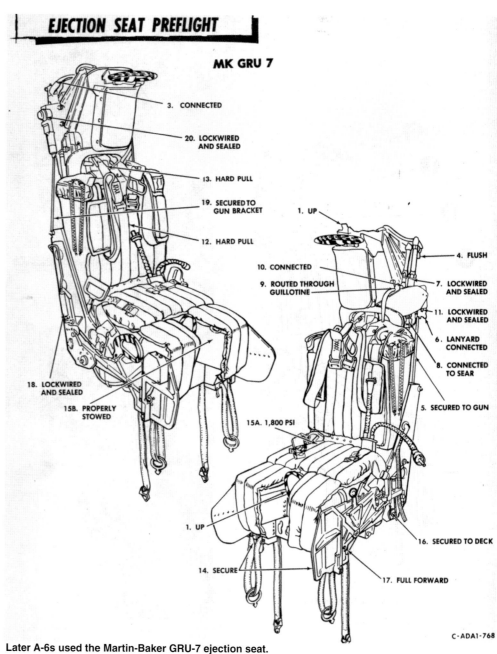

MK GRU 7

3. CONNECTED
20. LOCKWIRED AND SEALED
13. HARD PULL
19. SECURED TO GUN BRACKET
12. HARD PULL
1. UP
10. CONNECTED
9. ROUTED THROUGH GUILLOTINE
4. FLUSH
7. LOCKWIRED AND SEALED
11. LOCKWIRED AND SEALED
6. LANYARD CONNECTED
8. CONNECTED TO SEAR
5. SECURED TO GUN
18. LOCKWIRED AND SEALED
15B. PROPERLY STOWED
15A. 1,800 PSI
16. SECURED TO DECK
1. UP
14. SECURE
17. FULL FORWARD

C-ADA1-768

Later A-6s used the Martin-Baker GRU-7 ejection seat.

63

The pilot's side of the A-6E cockpit. The stick is in the foreground with the throttle quadrant to the left. The rudder pedals are on either side of the center console.

The pilot's side of the A-6E cockpit has a large vertical display indicator (CRT screen) that displays the primary flight instruments information. The radar altimeter is to the left and the barometric altimeter is on the right.

The top of the BN's seat. The Yellow/Black striped handle is the face curtain, which serves a dual purpose. When pulled out, it fires the ejection seat and it also protects the crewman's face from wind blast.

The pilot's optical reflector bomb/rocket sight on an A-6E. The A-6 has no Head Up Display (HUD) for the pilot.

The "coolie hat" on top of the stick controls lateral/longitudinal trim, while the Red button next to it is the bomb "pickle". Yellow button forward of the stick grip is the autopilot emergency disengage

The white handle forward of the throttle quandrant folds outward and when the throttles are full forward for catapult shot, the pilot grips this handle in addition to the throttles to keep the force of the cat shot from sliding the throttles rearward.

The magnetic compass is mounted on the canopy center support, as far away from the other instruments as possible.

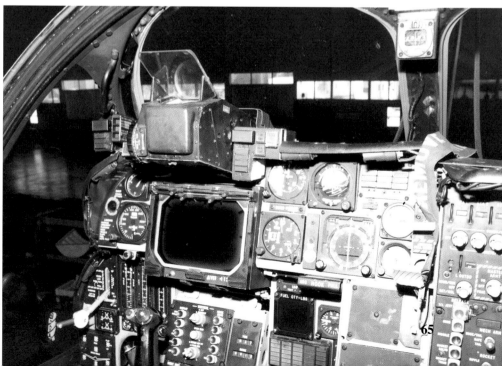

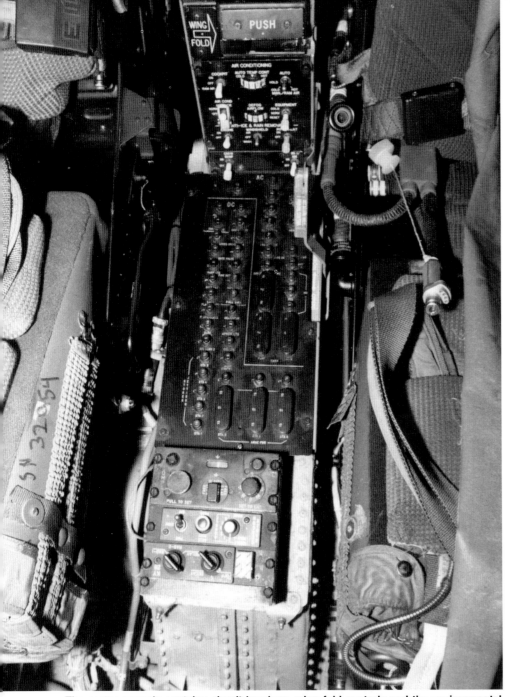

The center console contains circuit breakers, wing fold controls and the environmental system control panel (top center).

This console contains the autopilot controls (left center) and weapons control panel (right center).

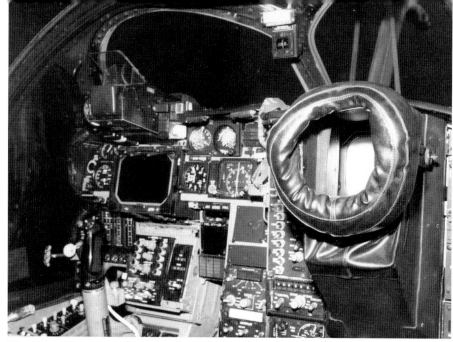

The radar screen that dominates the BN's panel can be covered by a large shroud to block out outside light reflections on the screen during daylight operations.

The stick in front of the BN's seat controls the radar and weapons system. The center and right consoles contain the ECM control panel, radar test panel, Doppler control panel and other electronics.

This control panel contains the Digital Display Unit (top) and BN's master control panel and INS controls. The small gauge is the outside temperature gauge.

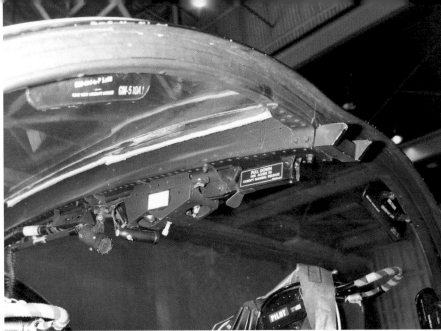

The canopy bow frame has two rear-view mirrors mounted on each side. The instructions on the canopy manual release state to "Pull Down For Access To Canopy Manual Release."

The small lights on the canopy center framing can be trained to illuminate maps, charts, checklists, etc.

The canopy center framing contains lighting controls and the manual canopy release lever.

The area behind the cockpit contains electrical junction boxes, a first aid kit, electrical conduits, hydraulic lines, the canopy hydraulic jack piston housing and the weapons monitoring unit computer. The rear canopy bulkhead is painted in Flat Black to reduce reflections in the canopy.

The canopy hydraulic jack actuating piston housing is in the center and the weapons monitoring computer is below it.

The canopy on the A-6 slides to the rear for entry. The separate canopies of the EA-6B raise upward. This EA-6B of VAQ-131 was aboard USS CONSTELLATION on 7 March 1994.

The A-6A assembly line in the Grumman factory at Calverton, Long Island, New York, during the early 1960s.

The open access panel on the inboard weapons pylon on an A-6E reveals the electrical connections for the pylon, wiring conduits, bomb/drop tank sway braces and fasteners.

The additional fairing on the outboard side of the outboard weapons pylon covers part of the wing fold mechanism.

This is the inboard pylon on an A-6A with all panels closed and fastened down. Each pylon has two sets of sway braces to help keep whatever is hung on the pylon from shifting.

The circular object between the sway braces if the ordnance rack attachment lug. In addition to bomb racks and weapons, the pylons have the necessary plumbing for fuel tanks.

The Multiple Ejector Rack (MER) is capable of carrying six bombs, three on the forward portion and three on the rear portion. It can be carried on any of the standard A-6 weapons pylons. The suspension lugs are in the center of the rack.

BNs perform a preflight inspection of the weapons load on A-6A Intruders of VA-165 aboard USS RANGER in the Gulf of Tonkin during January of 1968. The A-6 is carrying Multiple Eejector Racks (MERs) loaded with Mk 82 Snakeye high drag bombs on the outboard weapons pylons.

An A-6A of VA-85, with the wing pylons loaded with MERs carrying a total of twenty-four Mk 82 Snakeye bombs taxies toward the catapult aboard USS KITTY HAWK on 25 March 1967.

Ordnancemen load lowdrag bombs from a bomb cart onto an A-6A aboard USS RANGER during January of 1968.

This A-6A of VA-85 aboard USS AMERICA in the Gulf of Tonkin during June of 1968 has a message chalked on one of the Mk 82s. The aircraft also has a flak curtain installed in the BN's canopy.

These Red Shirts (Ordnancemen) are preparing to fuse the Mk 82s hung on the MER on this A-6A of VA-85. The 500 pound Mk 82 was one of the most widely used bombs of the Vietnam War.

The only weapon cleared for the EA-6B is the HARM anti-radiation missile. This EA-6B of VMAQ-2, returns to MCAS Yuma on 14 March 1992 after a captive training flight with a HARM missile.

This A-6E is loaded with a pair of AGM-88 HARM anti-radiation missile and twelve Mk 83 general purpose low drag bombs. The A-6E can carry a wide variety of weapons including rockets, missiles, cluster bombs, iron bombs and smart weapons.

A Boeing Military Aircraft Company aircrew evaluates 2.75 inch unguided rocket release during the contractor demonstration phase of the A-6E rewing program tests at NAS Patuxent River, Maryland.

An A-6 BN preflights a MER hung on the outboard weapons pylon which is loaded with six Blue twenty-five pound practice bombs.

An A-6 pilot checks to see that the pylon access panels have been properly secured as part of his preflight walk around.

This A-6A is loaded with two 300 gallon external fuel tanks on the inboard pylons. The A-6 can carry these tanks on all five pylons for a ferry mission.

This A-6 of VMA (AW)-224 is loaded with Mk 20 Rockeye anti-armor cluster bombs during Linebacker operations against North Vietnam on 7 May 1972.

An A-6 crwman checks the Mk 82s on his A-6 aboard USS EISENHOWER (CVN-69). The MER is loaded with only five on the inboard pylon since the sixth would not clear the landing gear door.

This was the A-6E TRAM prototype. The antennas under the nose are the VHF communications (forward), UHF communications (second long antenna) and TACAN (last short antenna).

A-6Es of VA-52 refuel from a KA-3B tanker. Prior to retirement of the KA-6D, each squadron had four or five tanker Intruders as part of their inventory. The shortfall in tanker capability was handled by the KA-3, until it too was retired. Current practice is to configure A-6 bombers with "Buddy" refueling stores on one or more stations.

An A-6E of VA-42 on final approach to NAS El Centro, California on 15 January 1994. It is configured with a "Buddy" refueling store on the centerline station.

An A-6E (VK-3 BuNo 155657) of VMA(AW)-121 at NAF Washington, during November of 1974. Except for the addition of some cooling scoops and a few new antennas, the basic shape of the Intuder has not changed in thirty years.

The final Intruder. The A-6F was built in prototype form only and, even though the A-12 project was cancelled, the A-6F was never funded.